Contents

DREAMWORKS

MADAGASCAR

ANNUAL 2006

Pedigree®

Published by Pedigree Books Limited
Beech Hill House, Walnut Gardens, Exeter, Devon EX4 4DH.
E-mail books@pedigreebooks.co.uk
Published 2005

DREAMWORKS
ANIMATION SKG

£6.99

MARTY

Marty the zebra is a dreamer. Bored with his life at the Zoo, he longs to get back to his roots. He wonders what life is like outside the zoo. Well, thanks to this eternal optimist, he and his friends will soon find out.

ALEX

Alex the lion was born into a life of privilege. He is the king of the New York Zoo, a true star in the greatest city on earth. He knows he can always count on his three pals. And that's a very good thing, because even a king needs friends.

GLORIA

Born and raised in the New York Zoo, Gloria is one hip hippo. She is beautiful, smart, practical and understanding. Her zoomates realise that she knows what she wants and how to get it. And she's always looking out for all of them.

MELMAN

Melman the giraffe is a hypochondriac who worries a lot about very little. Melman believes he's a real worldly guy. And compared to his three friends, he is.

THE PENGUINS

Skipper, Private, Kowalski and Rico may look like cute and cuddly penguins, but at heart they are a plucky, mischievous, take-charge bunch of die-hard adventurers. Their plan to escape from New York and head for the wide open spaces of Antarctica gives Marty the idea that there might be more to life than the zoo.

JULIEN

Julien, king of the lemurs, likes nothing better than to party, but his parties are often interrupted by fossa attacks. So when he realises that the fossa are scared of Alex, this cunning lemur sees the advantages of having a terrifying predator on his side.

MAURICE

Julien's sidekick, Maurice, has doubts about Julien's plan to befriend the 'New York Giants'. He points out that so far as Alex is concerned other animals are nothing but steak.

MORT

Attention-seeking Mort may be the cutest lemur in the universe, but Julien finds him so annoying he will jump at any opportunity to get rid of him for good.

A Bid for Freedom

Marty was in a state of bliss, running through an idyllic valley towards a beautiful lake, when he was jolted out of his fantasy by Alex the lion. "Surprise!" yelled Alex. Marty's daydream came to an abrupt halt and he tumbled off his treadmill in the zebra enclosure of the New York Zoo, "Aaaaah! Alex! You almost gave me a heart attack!" he gasped.

"C'mon Marty, I wanted to wish you a happy birthday! Hey, I got something stuck in my teeth. Can you help me out here?" Marty put his head in Alex's mouth and pulled out a present. It was a New York City snow globe with a miniature Alex perched on his rock. Marty gave Alex a half smile.

"You don't like it?" asked Alex. "No, no. It's just that another year has gone and I'm still doing the same things. Stand over here, trot over there, eat some grass..." Marty replied. "You just need to break out of the routine. Make it fresh!" Alex advised him, as the zoo opened for the day and people flooded into the park.

Alex leaped on top of Gloria the hippo, who was wallowing in her pool. "Let's go, Gloria, we're open!" he yelled. Gloria sank back into the water to sleep. Alex jumped onto the roof of the giraffe house. "Wake up, Melman, rise and shine," he shouted. "I'm calling in sick," said Melman, "I found another brown spot on my shoulder today."

Marty stretched and warmed up, "I'm going to be fresh. Freshalicious. Ziplock fresh," he said. As the announcer called his name, Alex climbed onto his rock and struck a majestic pose for the visitors. Fireworks erupted either side of him and the audience cheered.

In the penguin enclosure Skipper barked orders to the other penguins, "Smile and wave, boys!" Then he turned and yelled down a hole, "Kowalski! Progress report!" Kowalski popped up from the hole "We're only 500 feet from the sewer line, but we've broken our shovel," he said, holding a plastic spoon.

"Well, show's over, folks. I hope you thought it was fresh," said Marty. As his visitors walked away he saw a spoon burst from the soil in his pen. A hole opened up and four penguins appeared. "What are you guys doing?" asked Marty. "We're digging to the wide open spaces of Antarctica. To the wild!" Skipper explained.

"You didn't see anything," Skipper told Marty as the penguins dropped back into the hole, corking the entrance with an Alex Collector cup. Marty sank deep into thought as, behind him, Alex happily performed for the crowd. Finally, the clock chimed five and the visitors left the zoo.

That night, zoo workers delivered lavish platters of food to the animals. Then Gloria presented Marty with a birthday cake. "Let's make a wish, Babycakes," she said. Marty blew out the candles. "What did you wish for?" asked Alex. "I can't tell you. It's bad luck," Marty replied, taking a big bite of the cake.

"C'mon, tell," said Alex. Finally, after much persuasion, Marty gave in, "Okay, I wished I could go to the wild, back to nature, with clean air and wide open spaces. The penguins are going so why can't I?" Alex fell off the wall laughing. "I hear they have wide open spaces in Connecticut," Gloria told him.

When Gloria and Melman had gone to bed, Marty stared wistfully at the mural next to his cage. Alex tried to understand how Marty felt. "You're the best friend a guy could have. Are you going to go running off to the wild by yourself?"

Alex was dreaming of steak when suddenly he was woken by Melman, "It's Marty! He's gone!" Melman and Gloria stood in shock as Alex searched Marty's pen. "Where would he go?" asked Gloria. "Connecticut!" Alex replied giving her a grim look. "We gotta go after him. Which is the fastest way to Grand Central Station?"

Gloria smashed a hole through the zoo wall and they hurried to the subway. They boarded a train, and the passengers ran out screaming. When they got out at Grand Central, Melman's neck got stuck in the door. As he pulled himself free he crashed into a busker's drumkit and stumbled away with drums stuck on his hooves.

Meanwhile, Marty was strutting the streets of New York City. He was surprised to see someone who looked familiar.

Marty's hooves clicked on the marble floor of Grand Central Station which, at this hour, was almost empty. Suddenly there were screams from the escalator as Alex, Gloria and Melman made their way up from the subway. Marty was blind-sided by Alex. "What's the big deal?" he asked. "I was coming back in the morning."

The drums on Melman's feet skidded on the marble floor and he crashed into the information kiosk clock. He staggered around blindly as Gloria tried to pull the clock off his head. Suddenly they heard sirens and masses of policemen flooded into the hall, surrounding the four friends.

The animals were caught in the glare of the police searchlights. "Good evening, officers," said Marty with a big grin. "Hey, I'm going to handle this, Marty!" Alex said, as the police raised their riot shields.

"Hey, it's cool everybody, I'm Alex, from the zoo," Alex attempted to explain, giving a friendly growl. "We're just going to take my little friend here home and forget this ever happened." Suddenly, a tranquillizer dart hit him in the haunch and he fell to the floor.

To The Wild

Skipper and his penguin pals are determined to tunnel out of the zoo and head for the wilds of Antarctica. Follow Skipper's directions to find the escape route from their enclosure.

Start

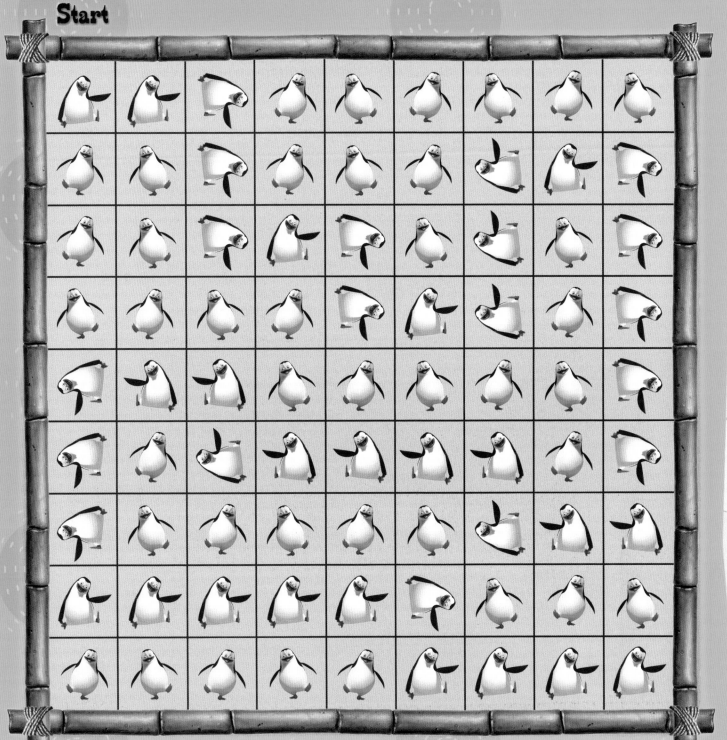

Finish

Solution on page 61

Sedated and Crated

The zoo animals are packed in their crates.
Can you work out which animal is in each
crate by looking through the air holes?

Odd Zebra Out

One of these pictures of our mono-chromatic friend is different to the others. Can you spot the stripe-a-licious stranger?

Answer on page 61

Back to Nature

"Ugh, my head," groaned Alex as he woke up in a shipping crate. "I'm in a box! I can't breathe! I'm so alone..." Then he heard a voice beside him, "Alex, are you there?" asked Marty. "Alex? Marty? Are you there?" shouted Gloria from below them. "Ugh..." moaned Melman, "Sleeping just knocks me out."

"Melman, are you OK?" asked Gloria. "Yeah, I often doze off when I'm getting an MRI," Melman replied. "It's not an MRI," Alex informed him, "It's a zoo transfer. It's because of you,

Kowalski stuck his head out of the penguins' crate and looked at the shipping label. "Progress report!" Skipper demanded. "It's an older code. I can't make it out," replied Kowalski. "You, higher mammal, can you read?" Skipper shouted. "Ship to Kenya Wildlife Preserve, Africa," read one of the chimps.

Rico coughed up a paper clip and picked the lock to the crate so the penguins could escape. They crept up to the bridge, where the captain was listening to music on headphones, and Kowalski knocked him out cold with a karate chop to the neck.

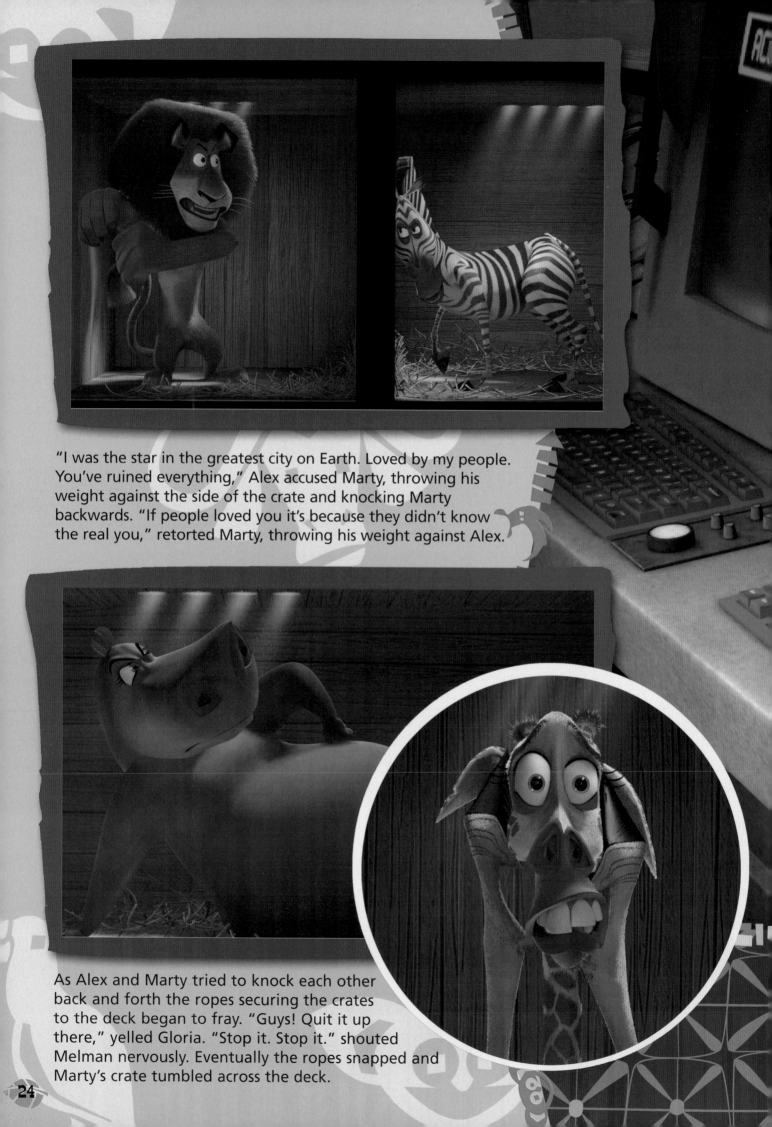

"I was the star in the greatest city on Earth. Loved by my people. You've ruined everything," Alex accused Marty, throwing his weight against the side of the crate and knocking Marty backwards. "If people loved you it's because they didn't know the real you," retorted Marty, throwing his weight against Alex.

As Alex and Marty tried to knock each other back and forth the ropes securing the crates to the deck began to fray. "Guys! Quit it up there," yelled Gloria. "Stop it. Stop it." shouted Melman nervously. Eventually the ropes snapped and Marty's crate tumbled across the deck.

On the bridge, Private was jumping on the computer keyboard, while the penguins tried to figure out where they were. "It's no good, Skipper, I don't know the codes," he said. Suddenly the message "Override Accepted" appeared on the screen. "Let's get this tin can turned around!" ordered Skipper.

The penguins jumped on the ship's wheel and it made a tight turn. Alex's crate slid into the chain railing at the edge of the deck, followed by Marty and Melman's crates. Alex saw a crate labelled Hippopotamus sliding towards him. The impact broke the chain and all four crates plunged overboard.

Alex peeked out of his crate to see the ship steaming away in the distance. "Marty? Gloria? Melman?" he yelled, but all he heard were the sounds of the ocean. Suddenly a huge wave washed his crate ashore and Alex tumbled out onto the beach. He ran backwards and forwards calling for his friends.

The next morning Alex staggered down the beach to find a tall crate, moving frantically. "Melman?" he shouted. Alex ripped open the top of the crate and tried to pull Melman out by the horns. Then he ran to get a log to ram Melman out. "Alex, wait! Wait! Hey, look it's Gloria," yelled Melman, in a panic.

Alex spotted Gloria's crate washed up on the beach. He knocked on the end just as Gloria kicked it open, sending Alex flying. He crashed down on Melman's crate, which broke, setting him free. Gloria climbed out wearing a crab and a couple of starfish.

The three turned to see Marty surfing to shore on the backs of two porpoises. Alex ran to greet Marty, then remembered their argument. "I am going to kill you," he roared. "Stop it. We're all here together safe and sound," said Gloria, hugging them all. "Where exactly is here?" asked Melman.

The friends looked round to see a massive wall of wild tropical jungle, lit by the morning sun. "San Diego," Melman declared. "White sandy beaches, cleverly simulated natural environment, complete with fake rocks." Marty took in the scenery, "This place is crack-a-lackin'! I could hang here..." he said.

"I'm gonna strangle you!" Alex yelled at Marty. "Now look," said Gloria, "we're going to find the people, get checked in and have this mess straightened out."

"San Diego! Now I'll have to compete with Shamu and his smug little grin. I can't top that, I'm outta the business. It's your fault, Marty. You've ruined me!" Alex moaned. He stopped short as they heard the sound of distant music drifting over the treetops.

The animals dashed towards the sound. "Where there's music, there's people!" said Gloria. Running through the jungle, Alex stubbed his toe on a rock, then stepped on a thorn. Bouncing on one leg, he hopped into a giant spider's web. He knocked into a tree, then tripped over a log.

Unaware of Alex's problems, the other three ran towards a huge baobab tree. They peered into the clearing to see a group of lemurs dancing wildly. "California animals!" exclaimed Melman, "I just saw twenty-six blatant health code violations. Twenty-seven!" he added, spotting another.

Marty was shaking to the music. "This place is fresh! I brought my hips! Let's dance!" He started to head towards the party, but Gloria held him back. "Where's Alex?" she asked. Suddenly the music stopped. "The fossa are attacking! Run for your lives!" shouted a lemur.

By the time Alex caught up with them, the clearing was empty except for four fossa surrounding Mort, a tiny lemur, who was being tossed in a salad bowl with mixed greens. The fossa froze at the sight of Alex, so Mort made a break for it.

"Hey... Hi..." Alex said to the fossa. "Um, we just got in from New York and we're looking for a supervisor because we've been sitting on the beach for hours and nobody's shown up." The fossa were terrified and ran off into the jungle. The lemurs, who had been hiding in the bushes, were astounded.

"Did you see that?" Julien, king of the lemurs, asked his sidekick, Maurice, pointing at the fleeing fossa. "King Julien, what are they?" gasped Mort. "They are aliens from the savage future," Julien declared, "but I have devised a cunning test to see whether they are savage killers," he continued, glancing at Mort.

Mort suddenly landed at the New Yorkers' feet. "Hi there," said Alex. Mort snivelled pitifully as he stared at Alex's sharp teeth. Gloria picked him up and they all talked baby-talk to him. "They're a bunch of pansies," Julien concluded. "C'mon, let's go and meet the pansies."

Lemurs rushed out from all directions to greet the visitors. Julien leaped onto the shoulders of a lemur, who jumped onto the shoulders of another. "Welcome, giant pansies," he said. "Thank you for chasing away the fossa, they are always annoying us by trespassing, interrupting our parties, ripping our limbs off..."

"That's nice," Alex interrupted him. "Look we just want to find out where the people are." Julien pointed to a skeleton hanging from a parachute high in a tree. "They're up there," he said, "not a very lively bunch though."

"So, do you have any <u>live</u> people?" asked Alex. "If we had live people here it wouldn't be called the wild," Maurice replied. Alex turned and ran towards the ocean. "I'm swimming to New York," he declared. Gloria held him back, "As soon as people realise what's happened they'll come looking for us," she reassured him.

Melman followed them out of the jungle, his head covered with vines, "Aaaagh!" he cried, "Nature! It's all over me! I can't see!"

Later Alex and Gloria stood over Melman, who had dug his own grave. Marty ran over to the group. "A latrine. Nice work, Melman," he said. "It's a grave. You've sent Melman to his grave!" Alex told him. "This isn't the end," Marty insisted, "this is a new beginning. This could be the best thing that's happened to us."

"No! No! No! You abused the power of a birthday wish and brought this bad luck on us all!" Alex yelled. "You guys made me tell you," Marty replied. "Besides, this is good luck. Look around you there are no fences, no schedules. Baby, we were born to be here."

"I've had enough of this!" said Alex drawing a line in the sand. "That's your side of the island and this is the side for those who love New York and care about going home." Marty tried to step over the line and Alex karate chopped the sand at his feet. "Okay," said Marty, "if you need me, I'll be here on the fun side."

The computer screen on board the ship read 250 miles south. "Well boys, it's going to be ice cold sushi for breakfast," Skipper told the other penguins. They high-fived each other and Rico popped open a bottle of champagne.

That evening, Melman rubbed two pieces of wood together, trying to start a fire, while Alex built a wooden structure resembling the Statue of Liberty. On the other side of the island, Marty was putting the finishing touches to his cabana. "She is finito!" Alex declared. "How's the liberty fire going, Melman?"

"I... I can't do it" Melman stuttered. He threw the boards down and they ignited. Realising they were still tied to his wrists he freaked out and staggered towards the statue, which was soon alight. Alex jumped from the top and landed face down. "You maniac!" he yelled. "Can we go to the fun side now?" asked Melman.

"Yo, Al," said Marty walking over to Alex, "Melman and Gloria are over there having a good time. There's room on the fun side for one more." Alex didn't even look up. "Marty, I'm tired. I'm hungry. I just want to go home," he replied wearily. "Why is everything always about what <u>you</u> want," Marty sighed.

Eventually, Alex went over to Marty's cabana. 'I'm sorry," he said, "if this is what you want then I'll give it a shot." Marty smiled. "Welcome to Casa del Wild," he cried.

Wild Wordsearch

This is no ordinary wordsearch. Before you can look for the words, you have to find the answers to the clues below. Remember, words can run backwards, forwards, up, down and diagonally.

```
B  U  K  G  R  C  S  Y  H  D
E  O  Y  A  N  D  K  O  J  N
M  E  L  M  A  N  I  W  C  L
L  V  J  E  O  D  P  Q  U  E
E  S  B  V  K  U  P  V  C  L
O  V  M  L  O  W  E  I  B  M
V  N  A  O  T  L  R  P  T  X
X  I  R  P  R  U  C  R  P  K
E  S  T  U  A  Z  I  E  L  M
L  M  Y  M  V  W  E  R  X  B
A  C  I  T  C  R  A  T  N  A
P  I  V  E  O  T  S  L  E  U
U  N  R  I  C  V  S  P  I  P
C  M  J  O  V  L  O  S  L  V
A  Y  S  V  L  N  F  Z  U  L
T  R  O  M  F  G  K  E  J  N
```

CLUES

1. The names of the four New Yorkers
2. King of the lemurs
3. The lemur king's second in command
4. The cutest lemur
5. Leader of the penguins
6. Where the penguins want to live (until they find out how cold it is)
7. The lemurs' arch enemies

39

Answer on page 61

Lurking Lemurs

The lemurs are hiding in the bushes, checking out the 'New York Giants' from a safe distance. How many pairs of eyes can you spot peering out from the jungle?

Answer on page 61

Crossword Crazy

Solve the clues below to reveal the
word in the centre column.

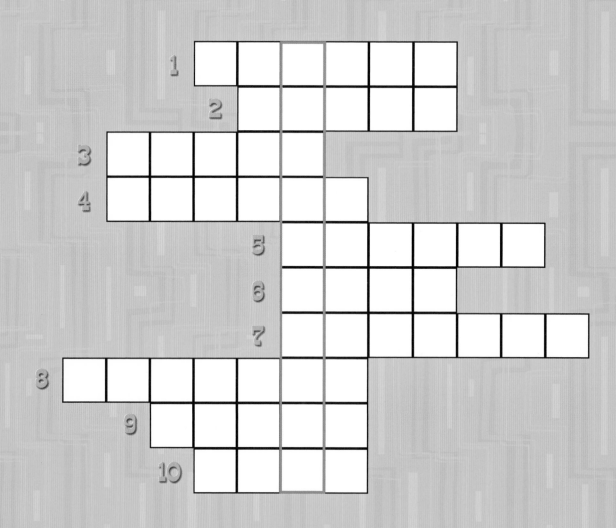

CLUES
1. The party animals
2. He's stripe-a-licious
3. The four friends were captured in _ _ _ _ _ Central Station
4. He's a long-necked hypochondriac
5. She's one happening hippo!
6. The cat!
7. Leader of the penguins
8. King Julien's sidekick
9. Alex dreams of this
10. He's small, furry and good with mixed greens

`Answers on page 61

A Walk on the Wild Side

The lemurs held a meeting in the wrecked plane up in the baobab tree. "For as long as we can remember we have been attacked by the dreaded fossa," Julien began, "So my genius plan is this – we make the New York giants our friends. Then, with Mr. Alex protecting us, we will never have to worry about the fossa again."

"Hold on everybody," Maurice interrupted. "Why were the fossa were so scared of Mr. Alex? Maybe we should be scared too." The lemurs looked concerned. "Maurice, you did not raise your hand, so we will strike that from the record," said Julien. "We'll make sure that the New York giants wake up in paradise."

Meanwhile, the penguins had finally arrived in Antarctica. It was bleak and icy, the wind was howling and snow was blowing sideways. "Well, this sucks!" said Private.

Back on Madagascar, Alex was dreaming of steaks. One landed on his chest and he licked it. He woke up to find he was licking Marty's haunch. Julien and Maurice were observing the New Yorkers from a tree. "You see, Maurice, Mr. Alex was grooming his friend," said Julien. "Looked more like he was tasting him to me," Maurice replied.

Alex was woken by Julien standing on his chest. "Good Morning!!"
Julien shouted as the lemurs cheered. Maurice blew a shell horn and
lemurs came rushing out with platters of fruit. "Where are we, what is
going on?" Alex yelled, jumping to his feet.

"Don't be alarmed, giant freaks, "Julien reassured them, "while you
were asleep we took you to our little corner of heaven. Welcome to
Madagascar!" The four friends turned to see an incredible vista, exactly
like Marty's mural back at the zoo. Marty grinned, "How about once
around the park?" he said, chasing Alex.

Marty and Alex swung on a vine into the clearing where a party was in full swing. Gloria lounged in the waterfall pool with a coconut cocktail. Lemurs were doing her nails and rubbing her back; others were giving Melman a neck massage.

"You see Maurice, my plan is working. Alex is our friend and the fossa are nowhere to be seen,' Julien boasted. "Alex, you should try some of this," Marty called, holding up a pineapple. Alex took a bite, then spat it out in disgust. "I feel good! I feel like a king again!" Alex said.

"You should see his act," said Marty, "c'mon Alex, why don't you show them your act?" Alex bounded onto the stage and struck a pose, while lemurs blew flower petals out of bamboo tubes, just like the fireworks back at the zoo in New York.

"Do the roar, man!" shouted Marty and, for the first time in his life Alex let out a huge lion roar. He threw his arms in the air and out came his claws.

Marty was oblivious to Alex's transformation. Suddenly Alex bit him on the butt. "What the heck is wrong with you? Why'd you bite me?" demanded Marty. "Man, it is because you are his dinner," Maurice told them. "What?!" Melman said.

"Your friend here is a deluxe hunting and eating machine," Maurice explained. "And he eats steak. Which is you!" Maurice continued, turning to Marty, Gloria and Melman. "We are all steak!" Julien added. Alex turned away in horror. When he looked back he saw a group of talking steaks

"Mr. Alex belongs with his own kind, on the fossa side of the island," said Maurice. Alex started chasing Marty, a wild look in his eyes. A coconut hit him on the head. "Excellent shot, Maurice," said Julien. Marty saw the reality of life in the wild, a world of predator and prey, where lions and zebras couldn't be friends

Alex is devastated, he cannot believe he was chasing his best friend. He realised he must leave that side of the island. When Alex arrived in fossa territory, he built himself a cage of wooden spikes, just like his cage back at the zoo, complete with his rock and a moat.

"What have I done? Because of me we've lost Alex," groaned Marty as they trudged through the jungle. "We're going to find a way to help him," said Gloria. "We're New Yorkers, right? We're tough!" They were interrupted by a "BRAAAP!!! "The boat's come back for us," Marty shouted and they ran towards the beach.

The boat ploughed onto the shore and ground to a halt. The penguins slid down onto the sand. "Now this is more like it," said Skipper. Melman and Gloria turned towards the jungle to find Marty had disappeared. "He's gone back for Alex! He'll get himself killed!" Gloria declared. Skipper stared into the jungle, "Well boys, looks like we have a job to do."

Marty walked along a jungle trail looking for Alex, unaware of the fossa gathering in the bushes on either side, watching hungrily as he passed. "Alex! Come out, Alex!" he shouted.

Alex dreamed he heard the crowds chanting his name. He woke to see Marty standing nervously at the edge of his enclosure. "Alex, the boat came back. We can get out of here – back to civilisation," Marty told him. "Stay back, Marty, please! I'm a monster" Alex replied, lunging towards him.

Alex turned away, horrified at what he had done and went back into his hut. Steeling himself, Marty squeezed between the bars of Alex's makeshift cage. "Alex, I ain't leaving without you," he said. Meanwhile the fossa were creeping down the rock walls and surrounding Marty.

Marty finally caught sight of the fossa. "Uh... Alex? Could you come out here for a minute? Alex, heeeeelp!" he shouted. Marty ran and the fossa chased him. The hungry fossa pounced on him from all sides. Then he heard a strange yell. Melman swooped down on a vine and grabbed Marty.

"Run!" yelled Gloria. The penguins joined the fight, but it was no use – they were out-numbered. Aloud roar brought everyone to a halt. It was Alex. "My kill!" he shouted, grabbing Marty, Gloria and Melman. Marty shut his eyes. "Psst. It's showtime," Alex whispered.

Alex faced up to the fossa. "This is my territory and I don't ever want to see you on this side of the island again!" he roared. The fossa fled in fear.

Back on the beach everyone celebrated at a Bon Voyage party for the New Yorkers. Marty proposed a toast and everyone sipped their seawater – then spat it out.

Skipper and Rico prepared a special meal for Alex – fish sushi. "Open the hatch. No peeking," Skipper commanded. Alex chewed and swallowed. "Delicious!" he declared.

Finally, the four friends climbed aboard the ship. "You know it's winter back home. Should we make a stop on the way?" Alex asked. "Paris!" Gloria cried.

Meanwhile, the penguins were sunbathing on the beach. "Should we tell them it's out of gas?" asked Private. "Why ruin a good party? Just smile and wave boys," Skipper ordered.

It's Quiz Time

How well do you know Madagascar??

1. What did Alex give Marty for his birthday?

2. What did the penguins use to cork the hole they made in Marty's enclosure?

3. Where did Marty plan to travel to from Grand Central Station?

4. What did Melman get stuck on his head at Grand Central Station?

5. What was Gloria wearing when she emerged from her crate?

6. How did Marty come ashore?

7. Where did Melman think they were when they first arrived on the island?

8. What did Julien and Maurice throw at the feet of the Zoosters to check whether they were savage killers?

9. What did Julien point to when the friends asked where the people were?

10. Who did the penguins refer to as 'our monochromatic friend'?

11. What did Skipper and Rico prepare for Alex to eat?

12. Where did Gloria want to stop off on the way home?

How did you score?

1-4

Totally illin'

5-8

You need to earn
your stripes

9-12

King of
the jungle

Find The Foursome

Only one group of jungle buddies exactly matches the four in the frame below. Can you hunt out the identical foursome?

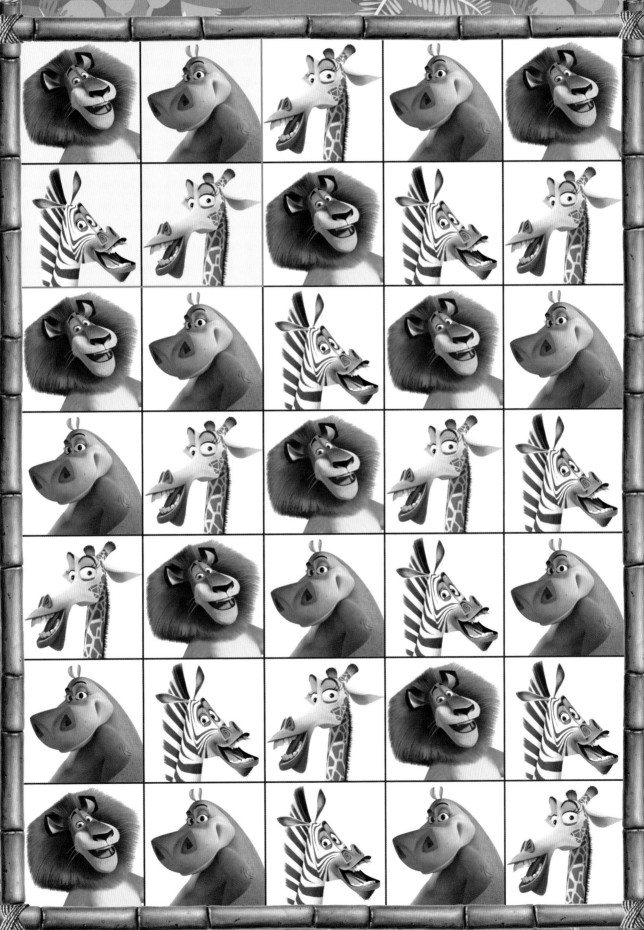

Hippo Happy Hour

Gloria's favourite cocktails to swallow while you wallow.

Cool Cat

75 ml orange juice
75 ml tonic water
A slice of orange or lemon
to decorate (optional)

Pour the orange juice into a tall glass, add some ice and top up with the tonic water. Serve with a slice of orange or lemon.

Orangatang

25 ml orange juice
25 ml pineapple juice
25 ml lemon juice
1 dash grenadine (optional)
50 ml soda water

Mix the juices together and add the grenadine, if using. Top up with soda water.

Sea Breeze

75 ml cranberry juice
75 ml grapefruit juice

Mix the two juices together and serve with ice.

Coconut Cooler

100 ml pineapple juice
25 ml coconut cream
crushed ice
pineapple slice for decoration

Shake or stir the pineapple juice and coconut cream together with the crushed ice. Serve immediately with the slice of pineapple.

Jungle Juice

30 ml orange juice
30 ml grapefruit juice
30 ml pineapple juice
10 ml grenadine (optional)
a lemon

Mix the juices together and add the grenadine if using. Add a squeeze of fresh lemon juiceand serve with ice and a slice of lemon.

Groovy Smoothie

2 ripe bananas
10 frozen strawberries
125 g carton vanilla yogurt
180 ml cold milk

Whizz all the ingredients together in a blender until smooth. Serve immediately.

Madagascan Mama

50 ml cranberry juice
25 ml orange juice
25 ml pineapple juice
25 ml ginger ale
lemon slices (optional)

Mix the juices together in a tall glass with some ice. Top up with the ginger ale and decorate withthe slices of lemon.

Hippopolitan

100 ml cranberry juice
25 ml orange juice
50 m grapefruit juice
a squeeze of fresh lime juice and a slice of lime

Mix the juices together in a tall glass with some ice. Add a squeeze of fresh lime juice and decorate with a slice of lime.

New Yorker

50 ml apple juice
15 ml blackcurrant cordial
25 ml double cream

Mix the ingredients together and serve chilled.

Gone Bananas

1 banana
25 ml orange juice
1 tsp clear honey
150 ml milk
Powdered cinnamon (optional)

Whizz all the ingredients except the cinnamon together in a blender until completely smooth. Serve immediately sprinkled with the powdered cinnamon, if using.

Chill Out Time

I banana
1 kiwi fruit
10 fresh or frozen strawberries
150 ml apple juice

Slice the fruit and whizz in a blender with the apple juice until completely smooth. Serve immediately.

Island Sunset

50 ml pineapple juice
30 ml grape juice
50 ml lemonade

Mix the juices together in a tall glass with some ice and top up with the lemonade.

Smells Like Steak

Alex has had his fill of fruit and is on the look out for some meat. Which trail will lead him to the steak he's dreaming of?

Answers

TO THE WILD (Page 19)

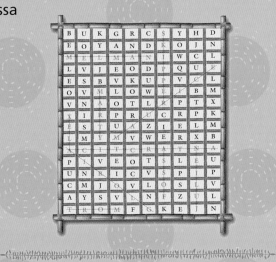

SEDATED AND CRATED (Page 20)
A. Marty the zebra
B. The penguins
C. Melman the giraffe
D. Alex the lion
E. Gloria the hippo

ODD ZEBRA OUT (Page 21)
E

WILD WORDSEARCH (Page 39)
1. Alex, Marty, Gloria, Melman
2. Julien
3. Maurice
4. Mort
5. Skipper
6. Antarctica
7. Fossa

LURKING LEMURS (Page 40)

CROSSWORD CRAZY (Page 42)

LEMURS
MARTY
GRAND
MELMAN
GLORIA
ALEX
SKIPPER
MAURICE
STEAK
MORT

IT'S QUIZ TIME (Page 56)
1. A snowglobe featuring a miniature Alex
2. An Alex collector cup
3. Connecticut
4. The clock from the information kiosk
5. A crab and two starfish
6. On the backs of two porpoises
7. San Diego Zoo
8. Mort, the mouse lemur
9. A skeleton
10. Marty
11. Fish sushi
12. Paris

FIND THE FOURSOME (Page 57)

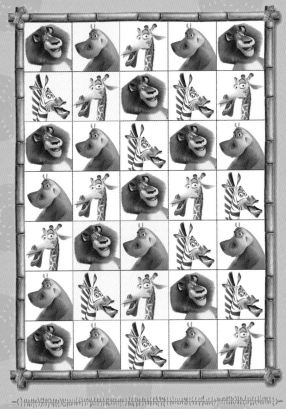

SMELLS LIKE STEAK (Page 60)
C

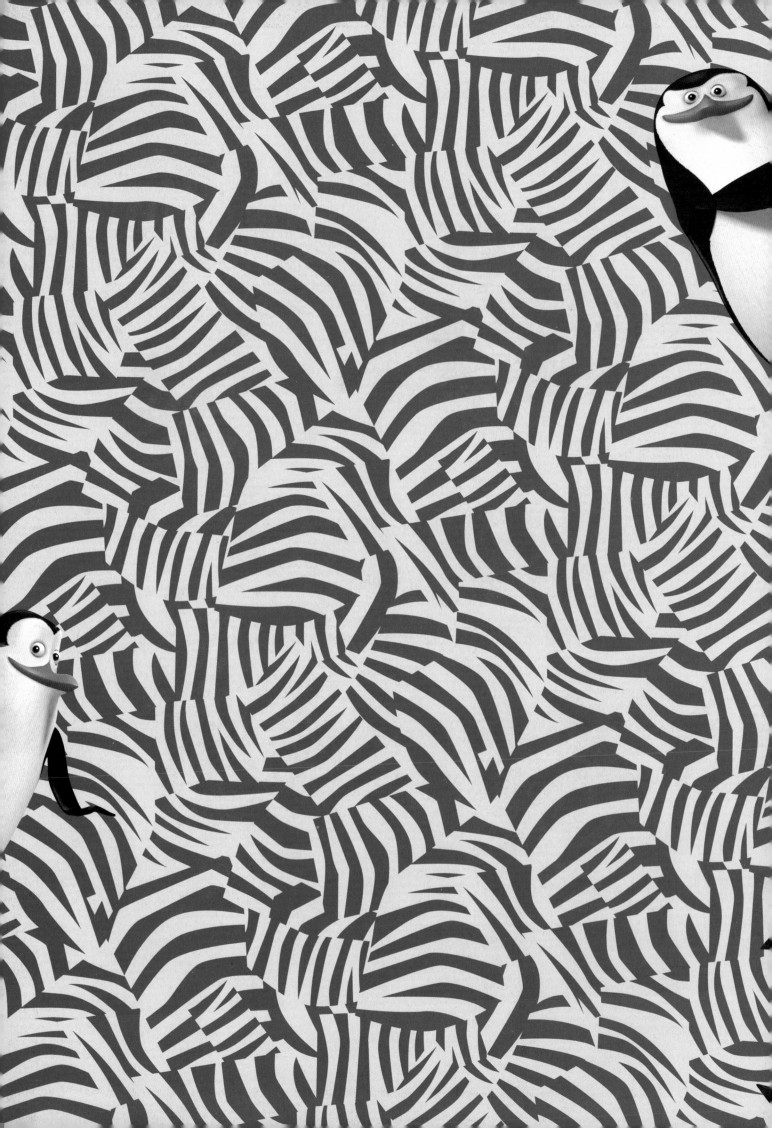